MW01503392

To my left

Love and love no more

Actions say it all

Nobody's perfect

What if? I would

Rewind

I'm asking

What hurts the most

Life

It's Over

In the night

Evening sky

Lying eyes

Bittersweet

Death becomes our youth

When it rains I see you

Two paths

Losing it all

what it takes to be a man

In the night

Solo

Hello Autumn

Moments

One on One

No regrets

Deceived

This too shall pass

A United Community

Just one wish

Sinner's salvation

Different approach

Dead in another's eyes

I have three siblings, 2 sisters and 1 brother,
and like most siblings we use to pick on each other.

As we got older my brother and I were the closest of us four,
since the last couple years it's not like that at all anymore.

Not because he is busy with his kids and wife,
but because of a bad choice I made in my life.

I got into the drug scene and got busted four years ago,
but I have long since let that past life go.

Nevertheless I have been branded a drug
addict in the eyes of my brother and his wife,
and they don't want me to be any part of their life.

They got married this last June I wasn't
invited because they didn't want me to go,
they have two girls 6 and 4 and a 5 month
old baby boy that I will never know.

All of us live in the same city just minutes away,
and all of usually got to my moms everyday.

Sadly I am not welcomed wherever my
brother or/and his wife go,
Devastated & Hated this hurts more
than anyone could know.

Happy 78th Birthday Grandma

*Happy birthday to a grandma who loves
everyone and someone who always cares,
and i know this through faith and
from her many prayers.*

*Love you Grandma 78 warm
wishes your way,
hope you have a wonderful and
happy birthday.*

Bitter Sweet

*You will always have my
heart without a doubt,
and you will always be the
one I can't live without.*

In all honesty we both know
forever won't happen for you and I,
its nice you say someday it will
but I know that's a lie.

I am happy knowing I am still apart of
your life even if it's just friends,
but behind this smile is a pain of
the love I have for you that will
never end.
Dedicated to Seven DFFD

How I see Poetry

Defining poetry is not
an easy thing to do,
there are many different
styles & different point of views.

I define poetry as a form of expression
of how the writer sees or how they feel,
a personal experience self expression
that's not fictional it's real.

personal experiences for me,
that's how i define poetry.

Shattered

Out of all the girls you know why did you come
into my life why did you have to choose me,
my heart was already disturbed not ready for this
again but somehow you bouight light and made me happy.

The last guy I trusted that lit up my life 4 years ago
I wasn't over until there was you,
I guess my trials & tribulations haven't ended & you
have no idea the hell I've been going through.

I'm stupid to think you could be different & help one
another to turn things around for the good,
now forgetting we ever happened or
the things you said I only wish I could.

Just like a guy you brushed us off like
I never really mattered,
and once again my faith & trust in
love has been shattered!

A Family of strangers

I was directed here from someone on another site,
he thought All Poetry would suit me just right.

AP has become my poetry family though

we've never personally met,
here there's no bad poetry or writes
everyone at AP is very considerate.

To have a place to go where you get some
acknowledgement on a piece you write,
gives confidence and a feeling of knowing
you are doing something right.

Everyone here at A.P.

I wanted to take a moment to let every
person here at All Poetry know,
how appreciative I am for the kind words
and helpfulness all of you show.

Through AP I have taken my poetry to a
different level that I am not a custom to,
writing something that is not personal
was something I didn't do.

Everyone here has different styles, great talent
and I'm thankful to be apart of this community,
so I just wanted to say thank you to
EVERYONE here at AP!

Just like you and I

Maybe people don't realize that deafness doesn't
make a person different from you or me,
here in Riverside, California there is a large
Deaf community.

Knowledge is what most lack on Deaf
Cultures and communities,
in life they have the same opportunities.

Beethoven was deaf and he wrote the best
classical music that is well known,
the original Incredible Hulk was deaf I'm
sure that was unknown.

Deaf does not make someone different
than you or I,
just a different language which isn't
hard to learn if you try.

Deaf Cultures and communities get
less awareness than it should,
they are a culture that is very easily
misunderstood.

Educate, learn have some knowledge you might
find it to be more interesting than you thought,
because being disabled or different from anyone
else deaf are not.

Unpredictable

I may wake up happy but that can
change throughout the day,

I may get irritated or if something
is not going my way.

Weeks can go by where
I'm just perfectly fine ,
then I'm crying emotionally
without a sign.

Girls are filled with so many emotions
that no man will ever understand,
like an oncoming storm not knowing
when we're going to land.

Author Notes
"I'm not a girl, I am a storm with skin." - Stir of Echoes
©. All rights reserved, 4 months ago

Her name is Princess Aurora

We all know her, but does everyone know her name?
she was a beauty abundant with gifts until the witch came.

Have you guessed who she is or do you still need time to think,
she has three little fairy godmothers and her dress is pink.

Sleeping Beauty is what most know her by,
she's one of my favorites, this is no lie.

Princess Aurora a name most of us have forgot,
but if you
ask me, I like her a lot.

If it is too hard to remember Princess Aurora,
remember her name rhymes with her fairy Flora.

Flora was in red, Fauna in green and Merryweather in blue,
now you know a little bit more so I hope you like
Princess Aurora as much as I do!

Outside my box

*My poetry are personal experiences and emotions I feel,
it's a chapter of my life and how I choose to deal.*

*I never written about something just out of the blue,
it never crossed my mind or had the need to.*

*So entering an AP contest helps me go outside the line,
a different experience that isn't all mine.*

What was it worth

We were friends for years before
she came along and into your life,
but who would have known you'd
be the one to stab me with a knife.

I never done you wrong if anything
helped you out so much more,
and yet you would throw me under
the bus for a cheating whore.

Then I hear she hacked into your facebook
and dragged your name in the dirt,
karma can be a real bitch, did what
she did to you bring on any hurt?

She has made your life nothing but a living hell,
happy to hear it's going very well.

I thought our friendship was worth more
than someone who will cheat and lie,
so was it worth it now that we have
said our final goodbye?

Love a deadly disease

I wasn't looking but somehow you found me,
I wasn't really interested so how could it be.

You were so persistent and you wouldn't expect a no,
I wasn't ready for where this relationship would go.

The most painful loss is a love that grows on you
when it's not what you wanted at all,
whatever you said whatever you did you
somehow made me fall.

You cheated we broke up that was four years ago,
why is it taking so long to let you go.

I tried everything I could to get you out of my head,
but your are the first thing i think about and the last before i go to bed.

Relationships don't work because it's not you and
I'm ruined I hope you know,
it's going to take the death of
hope to let you go.

Dedicated to Seven DFFD

Sought out suicide

Jenni was a fun loving girl who
was full of life and everyone's friend,
at the end of 2007 her relationship
with her boyfriend came to an end.

It was the day after new years when she found

out she was expecting and word got around fast,
shortly after she was back with her ex and
most of us knew it wouldn't last.

He promised her the world his world
would be hers for eternity,
but the time for them wasn't
right to have a baby.

Pondering the thought of an abortion she
wanted to hear opinions, some more insight,
I told her there were many options,
abortions I'm against it just ain't right.

Soon came rumors he was going to leave
her after the abortion was done,
I brought it to her attention
and I wasn't the only one.

She got it done anyway,
he left her the next day.

She warned people about
her thought of suicide,
there was nothing she was
trying to hide.

It was late Monday afternoon her employer
called saying she never showed for work that day,
she had hung herself in the garage with a 3 page
letter she left saying what she wanted to say.

This was in February 2008 four months
shy of her 21st birthday,
sad that not one but two lives
were taken away.

Such a sweet young girl,
no she never cried,
and never thought twice,
her sought out suicide.

Author Notes
Jennifer Lynn Pardo
6/5/1987 - 2/112008

Right kind of Wrong

He is who my heart will always desire,
but we are like gasoline and fire.

I know he's never going to settle down,
so why do I continue to come around.

I want him, I hate him, he's just stringing me along,
he'll leave me crying but he's my right kind of wrong.
Dedicated to Seven DFFD

It was all a dream

My first heartbreak was devastating,
I thought the hurt would never die.
Nobody could tell me otherwise,

they just don't want to see me cry.

With time you begin to heal,
and you start to see things more clear.
He's not hurting for you while
you just weep and weep lying here.

It hurts right now but
you will be able to move on too,
then you'll see he wasn't
good enough for you.

Guys will come guys will go,
but they will weep what they sew.

First Halloween

Mommy is dressing me up
like an angel I'm in all white,
we get to go door to door

getting free candy tonight.

We take pictures outside
in the yard before we leave,
then mommy goes and grabs
us all a long sleeve.

Some houses have pumpkins
with different shapes and faces,
some houses look spooky and
mommy don't want to go to those places.

I want a lot of candy
so I ask mommy why,
she said those houses
will make me cry.

I should have listened to
mommy that house is mean,
mommy says it will be OK
it's just my first Halloween.

My bag is getting too
heavy for me to carry,
and there is a lot of people
that are dressed scary.

I want to eat some of my candy
but mommy said I have to wait,
we start to head back home because
mommy said it's getting late.

I'm getting tired and
don't want to walk anymore,
mommy says OK this is
the last door.

Mommy kisses me says
it's time to go to bed,
Halloween is over and
takes the halo off my head.

When I wake up I'm going
to see what candy I got,
that bag was heavy so I
know there is a lot.

Renewed Rivalries

They took to the field Cowboy territory,
these rivals have a little bit of history.

Though they were in Dallas the
stadium was full of red & gold,
and oh the excitement to watch
this game unfold.

Interception after interception
good job Romo,
who plays for Dallas in case
you didn't know.

I am a big 49er fan and I loved
every minute of this game,
if I was a Dallas fan I would
feel so ashamed.

We wrangled over the Cowboys,
we'll be home to take on the Bears,
in my opinion I think it is an easy win
for these players!

Tatted mom

I remember the first one it is on the
back side of my left shoulder,
she used a few different colors but
the green was much bolder.

Orchids my favorite flower was
my very first tattoo,
since then I've gotten more
than a few.

Each represents a love or something
special to me,

my kids name in a banner around a
locked heart because they hold the key.

A cross for my grandfather who passed
away four years ago,
we were very close I still miss him so.

From the top of my left shoulder down
to my calf,
images of flowers cover that half.

I have one that covers my lower back and
one around my ankle on the right,
I even have a set of lips that glow in the
black light.

So it is easy to see how
Tatted mom became,
my one and only and reason
for my nickname.

A Connection through words

His words he writes, I know all too well.
He calls himself Mr Rebel.

He writes of love he once had,
and for him I feel bad.

I can see and feel his pain and I
can easily relate to,
but it's only a connection through
words that I know you.

Mr Rebel he calls himself would
be my favorite poet,
because i feel like I know him through
words does he show it.

Who I Am

Who I am is not in my
name that was given to me
and only a small perception
of what you see.

the things that matter most
are permanently on my skin,
but I have deeper thoughts and
feelings I keep within.

my poetry is where the real
emotion comes out,
happy, sad ,heartbroken or
just filled with doubt.

who I am, a mother of two who has
strong emotions that I don't express,
but here in my poetry is where
I do it best.

Close your eyes

standing on the edge of water and land
waves pushing over my feet along with sand

the wailing wind is dying down
sighing, alone, i look around

you're not here, that's no surprise
yet tears start to fill my eyes

my love for you, you have never missed

pleading with myself, because you don't exist

closed are my eyes while i'm lying in bed
this was just a dream that was in my head

Heavens Guardian

sweet little angel so peaceful and still
her guardian is his to fulfill

fierce like a lion but gentle as a lamb
her protector is what i am

the lamb of god, tiger to your eyes
her best friend in the heavenly skies
Author Notes
picture prompt contest

Behind the door

Behind that closed door
is something we've waited for

vivid colors, bright, warmth of the sun
the season of a sandy waterfront fun

summer awaits us, let's wait no more
and take part of what's behind that door

Beyond words mean

A feeling so deep and beyond strong
an emotion some search for so long

to give your own life, so the other may not feel pain
give beyond means with nothing to gain

love is more than an emotion, beyond what words can say
love is my children and it grows with every second everyday

Wrong Blonde

Women to women you have to hear me out
you have the wrong blonde, without a doubt

you know all "us" blondes we look alike
I like being tan, but this environment I dislike

there are more vindictive women that should be here in my place
someone made a terrible mistake and that's a disgrace

I don't condemn you for being down here
I just want to make that clear

I am not saying I am a perfect saint because that wouldn't be true
can we come to an agreement and send me to heaven in the skies blue

Love has no boundaries

She can't live out of the water,
he belongs to the skies
yet neither matters,
love is all they see in each other's eyes

she only cares how she feels when she's with him
she doesn't care he can't swim

he believes she owns the stars and the sky
he knows she can't fly

together, she's flying to his arms and he's swimming to her heart
love has no boundaries and nothing can keep them apart

Behind her smile

Everyone has something,
good or bad weighing on their mind
sometimes you can see that emotion
with others it's hard to define

the tears she sheds nobody sees
alone, by herself she cries with ease

a wrong path she chose to take
trying to be forgiven for her mistake

losing everything,
struggling to get it all back
outcast by family,
trying to stay on the right track

with time, it's easy to hide the tears
losing her struggle, is what she fears

in the public eye, she smiles and stands strong
behind that smile, tears of pain belong

Cold as Ice

I wasn't looking for love when he found me
how was I to know i would fall so easily

there was no love at first sight
nor did it happen over night

yet with every moment passing by
I was on the greatest high

at my highest point it all came crashing down
I had learned he was messing around

He is the one I compare everyone to
my heart is his no one else will do

Love is a fairy tale , a myth, unfair and it's not all nice
it's been five years and I still love a man as cold as ice
© . All rights reserved,
Dedicated to Seven DFFD

Summer Love

The long hot days brought on by the sun
down by the river with friends having fun

cold drink in my hand,
tanning on the sand

It is a time when people find a summer fling
a sense of pure freedom to do anything

warm summer nights with midnight dips in the river
who wants winter, always being cold makes you shiver

board shorts and fashionable bikinis is my favorite attire
you never have to try getting warm by a fire

my love is summer and all it has to bring
it's the best part of spring

spring gets you ready for those warm summer days
I love summer in so many ways

Look who's turning 4!

Hari, by your dad you must be so adored,
He is so excited that his son is turning four.

I bet you are excited and can't wait till your big day,
I'm sure you'll have cake balloons and lots of gifts coming your way.

May your day be filled with family and friends
Wishes and memories that never ends.

I'm sending you early wishes your way
And wishing you a Happy 4th Birthday!

Looks can be deceiving

Looks can easily be deceiving,
and possibly have you believing

Even the sweetest of us may have a dark side
We all have at least one secret to hide

Just as every rose has thorns
Some halos are held up by horns

Remember this, the devil was once an angel before
Looks can be deceiving need I say more.
Dedicated to Seven DFFD

Foolish Pride

We met when we were five then she moved away
a few years later she moved back to stay

She spent all her teenage years living with me
inseparable, I was even in the room when she had her baby

In between the ages of 17 and 18 things just weren't the same
one of us had changed but neither would take the blame

Shortly after she packed up all her things,
we were done and she moved away
one day out of spite i told her that her boyfriend cheated,
that call was made on her wedding day

Now we are older and many things have changed since then
young minds with foolish pride but 29 years she's still my friend
©. All rights reserved, 3 months ago

2015

The day is coming closer of a brand new year
with all my luck I didn't think I'd make it here.

The economy has been a little rough
which made this year for me tough.

With every slamming door in my face I still haven't gave in
so I know that in 2015 it's going to be my turn to win.

There's only Two

My heart and soul has already been taken, you see
only two very special people hold the key.

One my daughter holds, and the other held by my son
it was only them that my heart naturally won.

I know our love will never run,
even in times that aren't so fun.

A child's love is all I will ever need
and with my love I know they will succeed.

No man can ever win the key to my heart it's already done,
by the only two my daughter and my son

Untitled

You made it to 2015!
2015 is finally drawing near,
and look how fast it got here.

Being a single parent can be tough,
but for your little one that's more than enough.

You may think you don't have the best for your daughter/or son,
but to your child you're their world, their number one.

Enjoy every moment and thank God for helping you get here,
and have a Blessed Christmas and another blessed New Year.

Vengeful Scorn

Only a man can turn a woman so cold
by deceit and untrue words that were told

she gave her heart, he had it all
and in the end she felt so small

she thought the feelings were mutual, from what he would say
when it ended it was obvious the feelings were only one way

he knew how she felt, strung her along then left her torn
for he is the reason she has a vengeful scorn

she's lost all trust and respect for any guy
she learned from the best, knows every lie

behind the pretty eyes and that sweet smile
she wears a different profile

she wasn't always a devil in disguise
that was before the heartbreak and lies

because she once loved and lost
but look what it cost

Author Notes
Prompt contest
Dedicated to Seven DFFD

Dark Love

I would give up my life for you
there's nothing that I wouldn't do

I loved you and I think I
made that pretty clear
and it's because of what you
did that brought me here

what I thought was truth was
just your beautiful lie after lie
the only way for me to be sane
again at peace I would have to die

you play innocent in the games you play
that's what helps you get your way

I couldn't love again if I ever wanted to
because of what you fucking put me through

I wish I never had a heart to care
and you act like you are unaware

just go on about your life and
never look back again
you are more than a lethal kind of sin

you put me in a dark place,
I love no more
you're the type of person
that's rotten to the core

if you even care don't you
ever come around here again
that would be the nail in the
coffin that would do me in

The devil took more than my soul

His colors are black and red,
he sports a red devil head.

looking for someone, looking for his next prey
out of nowhere he just appeared one day

I had no interest I wasn't looking for no man
he was quite persistent and that's how it began

with all the time we spent together it was easy to see
I was drawn to him, falling in love, he knew he had me

soon our time together was now being spent apart
time with other girls now that he had my heart

He always came around, but he wasn't alone
but he's a Diablo, maybe I should have known

he will never be a one woman man, he'll never settle for one
yet I still love him, nothing can compare it can't be undone

there is nothing to hate which makes things hard
because of him I am forever scarred

it has been five years now since that devil stole my heart
had me higher than the stars then emotionally tore me apart

I've gone months with no contact went away to clear my head
yet over and over back to him is where i was lead

I've tried to find love but no one compares, for the damage has been done
he has left me breathless and still want more, the devil has won

Dedicated to Seven DFFD

Pay it forward

People today need to show more kindness and care
this is a different kind of lottery if you have a heart to spare

it's a state lottery, but there are no numbers to choose
if you like to give then this lotto you can't lose

do you know someone who is in need of, whatever it maybe
your lotto would be the name of your nominee

what they are in need of, like a house or a car
and for you, your name will become a star

a star will be named after you if your nominee has won
and the money collected will be invested for the need of your chosen one

My favorite sin

He'll never settle down, he's not a one woman man
I learned the hard way, when I should've just ran

I didn't want anyone at that time, I had no interest at all
he was persistent, how did I know that I would fall

that was five years ago yet we still hook up every once in awhile
he tells me some day soon, but I already know his style

the most painful thing about it all, I never told him how I feel
just on paper but no to his face, it's not easy when love is real

I have tried and tried, but in reality I don't think I ever will
because in reality I know that is not the way he feels

Author Notes
Loving you is wrong contest
Dedicated to Seven DFFD

Surreal

My love for him is eternal, there is no other for me
to think this is the last of you i'll ever see

it's hard to swallow it can't be true
nothing to ever look forward to

i can't breathe i'm choking back tears
this can't be how it appears

i'm shaking with the thought of losing you
nauseous weak i don't know what to do

breathless spinning i'm about to faint
this picture i can not paint

Not over him

Five years ago not looking but he was persistent. He grew on me, I fell
in love, he broke my heart and I'm still hurting.

what could it hurt

when you hit a dead end on every turning path and road you take
you've passed the point of rock bottom and you're about to break

it may not be what you believe,
but it's time to hit your knees

faith may not be what you believe or even care much for
but if you pray to God he will show you the open door

what could it hurt to believe in someone that could change how you feel
to have some faith and open your heart , what's it going to kill

you have endured so much and haven't gave up from what i know
and those who wronged you will one day reap what they sow

To the Unborn

I have a million things playing in my mind
how could someone I love be so hurtful and unkind

how can someone kill a baby who doesn't have a choice
something so innocent and fragile who can't speak their own voice

it changes your entire world when it's done by someone you know
it's a choice so heartless to let such a little life go

how can society make one killing okay and not the other
you can kill an unborn baby but be punished for killing your brother

there's contradiction in there we need to open our eyes and see
abortion clinics help murder thousand unborns, someone's' family

The unborn don't get a choice, but people kill people every day
we call them murderers and they are sent to jail to stay

but what about the unborn what kind of justice do they receive
just a careless girl who goes about with no grief

my prayers go out to all of the unwanted unborn
i will see you in heaven where i will no longer mourn.

"Dedicated to my niece or nephew whom never had a chance and i never
got to meet, i will see you in heaven. ~xoxo~
Author Notes
this is the first time I have published this poem publicly, I wrote it after
my sister had an abortion it was a hard time in my family, but this was
9 yrs ago and all has been forgiven and this has been put behind us until
we meet in heaven

For my sanity

Everyday it's go, go, go
I need to relax and take it slow

so I'm taking my kids, my only suitcase and leaving town
gather my thoughts and put my feet back on the ground

a couple bathing suits and a couple outfits for each of us
I don't care if we have to leave here by the bus

we're heading to the river to relax in the sun
enjoy the warmth, the water and have some fun

leave the worries and stress of home behind
we need some family time and just unwind

no worries about the time of day
doing whatever comes our way

a vacation it what we need just my son daughter and I
because i was ready to lose my sanity and that's no lie

Mother Moments

My mom doesn't have riches in money and fame
but I love her no matter what just the same

Every day is not perfect, but it's another day we are here
every moment is precious, our time on earth is unclear

there is no one special moment for me
Every day she's here I'm happy

My mom has helped or has done everything for me
I wouldn't know what to do without her
She is my world and I love her
but she's not told that enough that's for sure

Author Notes
contest happy moments with mother

Reannon

Reliable when asked to be
Effort to make everyone else happy
An older sister of two sisters and one brother
Not like any other

Need to have her own space
Often feels out of place
Never shows emotion always has the same face
Author Notes
acrostic poem contest

Only in the movies

Dancing under a starlit sky with him
the moon acting as our spotlight
getting that adrenaline kind of rush feeling
I know it's going to be a memorable night

just before we are about to kiss
we fall into each other's eyes
and no sooner than when our lips touch
thunder and lighting fill the skies

this night just got a whole lot better
wet from the rain things get more intense

not stopping but going for shelter
and losing all common sense

he picks me up and carries me inside
we start stripping of each others clothes,
this is my fantasy, and you know how the end goes!

Author Notes
a contest about your fantasy
Dedicated to Seven DFFD

Then I woke up

Sitting around the bonfire at night
me, wrapped in your arms so tight

listening to a slow country song
together is where we belong

you softly whisper to me
you love the way my green eyes gleam

61

before we kiss I wake up,
it was all just a dream.

Author Notes
contest 50 words on dreams

April 7th

In about 30 minutes, I will be 35
I sit here and I start to realize

I wasted my life over the last five years
I have cried an ocean of tears

still feel all alone struggling with no help from anyone
feeling hopeless about getting back my daughter and son

never has anything in life ever gone my way
worst of all, I lost my kids 5 years ago on my birthday

Poison

He's a devil with no disguise,
a snake with green eyes

a drug that you crave
he'll make you misbehave

he's a smooth charmer & no good in so many ways
he'll be around for a little while, then gone for days

I had a big heart I thought we'd be together when we're old
but the only thing he did was turn my heart cold

he's all that I want, but he will never be a one woman man
he's poison killing me slowly if I could go back before we began
and change my answer so I would never fall
I'd do it in a heartbeat & change it all

What am I

This is something that people make
it doesn't have to be held for it to break

it could hurt, but never touch you
it's just what some people do

sometimes it's intentional & sometime's
it's forgotten about

so do you think you know, have me figured
me out

It gets broken with kids and relationships to
it's something many too often do

do I still have you guessing what "it" is
in these words that I say
well I'm not going to tell you, you'll figured it out
somehow some way.....

Author Notes
prompt #2
riddle prompt © Reannon Smith. All rights reserved, April 9th, 2015

A new day

The first sight of the morning glare

The smell of fresh dew is in the air

the cool crisp weather of the early morning light
to the East the sun rises so boldly and bright

nothing but clear blue skies above
the still peacefulness, what's not to love

a big, long stretch and just one last morning yawn
with the sound of landscapers mowing neighbors lawns

small birds in a tree chirping a song
I love the morning, but they don't last long

Author Notes
rhyme

Curiosity killed the cat

Would you like to play a game with me
talk to those who you no longer see

you know, black cats are only
bad luck if they run in front of your car
so don't be scared,
have no fear and come as you are

it's just a game, what could go wrong?
just ask a couple questions, it won't take that long

it's not evil don't believe none of that

even if curiosity did kill the cat

Author's Notes
picture prompt

A thin line between love and hate

I remember it all too well
a time when life was hell

he was the best bullshitterI have ever met
and what I lost I haven't completely got back yet

it all started after we moved in together
his true colors started to weather

lying and cheating then just got worse from there
turned all my family against so I couldn't go anywhere

then it got physical but knew how to not leave a mark
the honeymoon was over things got very dark

he pushed me until I knew I could take no more
I couldn't be knocked down to the floor

I had to stand my ground it was time to fight back
no more could I let myself get smacked

coward is a man who beats on girls so they can feel tall
and that's what he was, now that I wasn't so small

but I couldn't leave I had nowhere to go
already being evicted, I had to do everything alone

we stayed with his mom until I found a place where I could move in
but my battle wasn't over, this wasn't quite the end

he had to take me down one more time to prove he was stronger
weak and defeated I wouldn't last much longer

finding himself a new love I thought I was free from my hell
wrong! hours after he moved out I was raided and took to jail

for something intentionally left behind
I had no knowledge, but the house was mine

that was five years ago and I still haven't made everything right
but I hear he still sleeps well every night

there is a thin line between love and hate
now I'm very choosy on the men I date

Black and white

So innocent with no knowledge of hate
hoping they don't grow up with that trait

if asked to anybody what color do you see?
most would say back and white, do you agree?

but a photo taken in black and white, would there be a color then?
so can you see now the message this photo is trying to send

we are not here to be divided by color
but to love and respect one another

Author Notes
picture prompt
© Reannon Smith. All rights reserved, April 13th, 2015

My Foundation

Where would I be without her,

without her love and nurture

she gave me life and I never had to go without

she stood her ground when I would pout

she gave me three siblings but only one was a brother

but she loved us all equally never one more than the other

there is nothing like a mother's love and everything they do

mothers are the hardest working people and under preciated to

you do so much and get so little you deserve more than a day

you should be celebrated the entire month of may

either way you do so much and I appreciate ALL that you do

Happy Mothers Day mom and always I love you

© Reannon Smith, a month ago

There was an old woman

There was an old woman who lived in a shoe

it stunk so bad she did not know what to do.

so she grabbed some pretty glitter and gave it a swill

colored it pink and now she has a beautiful high heel

© R. Smith, a month ago
nursery rhyme twisted prompt

Right kind of wrong

I never steered off the straight-line

that was before I called you mine

love will have you throw caution to the wind

knowing what we were doing was a sin

praying that we wouldn't end up like the rest

then that night we got it all off of our chest

I never imagined as far as I could see

even when you promised you'd never leave me

now looking back, so long ago I'm so glad we intertwined

because all these years, you're still the best thing that is mine

The words of my father

He was always the stern one & I

always thought he was mean,

he worked and slept so he was

the parent that was behind the scene.

The words he told me growing up

& are branded in my head

I often repeat those words he

always said.

He grew up in a home that didn't show any emotion

and his home never had any commotion

our home was far from what he grew up in

so his patience easily wore thin.

growing up the one thing my dad mostly told

was to use my common sense, a phrase that never

gets old.

he taught that trust had to be earned & that life wasn't fair

being so young what did I care

now that I am older I appreciate my parents so much more

Because I now understand what they tried to teach me before my dad may still not show much affection, but says I love you

and that is the best thing a father can say or do

When I'm gone

Just as I use poetry to express how I feel

he uses lyrics to express his ordeal

a moment in life when reality hits you

seeing the whole picture from an outsider point of view

knowing there is only tragedy if you continue this way

so put it in lyrics and let the radio play

the lyrics express the road you are currently on

and so much guilt that's building on

wondering if they'd be better off if you were gone

and they can just look up, smile and carry on

but as a parent it's not that easy to let give up and go away

because it would only kill you if you couldn't stay

Added May 12

song prompt "when I'm Gone" - Eminem

Love gone wrong

In a world that is full of lust,

love is only lost in the dust

one girl who was his world or at least she thought

she was purely in love but he was not

he made her feel special like she was the only one

but she would soon find out things are going to come undone

a night you've been planning all month just for you two

in the bedroom a dozen white roses but they aren't meant for you

written by him a love letter for someone he

expressingly cares so much about

hurt in a rage your life torn apart clenching

to the flowers head filling with doubt

with the roses clenched firmly in your hand

you put a bullet in your head

thinking he will forever be consumed with guilt

now that you are dead.

The strong & the weak

Hate is so common it preys on the weak

it's not easy to turn the other cheek

Love does take courage love is not easily done

it takes patience and work it's not all fun

courage comes from taking a chance on someone

with the possibility of getting hurt

sometimes people can be cruel string you along

then leave you in the dirt

there is no effort on hating

you put effort in dating

weak is to hate , it doesn't require anything at all

strong is the one who loves and takes the fall

© Reannon Smith, a month ago

If everyone cared

She wakes up every morning and dresses herself for school

trying to hide the bruises, but who is she trying to fool

she meets a new friend on the playground by the tires

but her new friend notices that she is a liar

the other kids and teachers know, but they look the other way

after school her new friend tells her dad what had happened that day

with tears in his daughter's eyes

how can he explain why her friend lies

the next school day he walked his daughter to the classroom

walking in he learned the news , while his girl wonders why

everyone's so gloom

as he kneels down to tell her a tear falls from his eye

as he tries to speak saying her friend will never lie

her new friend now has wings and can fly

up in heaven with Jesus in the sky

sadly no one cared enough to report was was going on

and it was too late way before the morning dawn.

Unfortunately, this song is a true story about an encounter his daughter

had

and teachers knew she was being abused but didn't say anything and

that's pretty sad

never is there any time in the world that child abuse is ok

and if more people cared more children would be alive today

© Reannon Smith, a month ago
song prompt, Alyssa Lies by Jason Michael Carroll

"Must Read"

Today I saw the most gorgeous sunset, but it couldn't compare

to the beauty of you, but it would have been perfect if you were there

Last night I saw the brightest star lit up in the skies

and it made me think of the sparkles I see in your eyes

No matter where in the world you ever are

know that my love for you can travel that far

if you ever think that nobody cares, you're wrong because I do

if ever at any time, anywhere know I am always here for you

© Reannon Smith, a month ago

Not his Cinderella

To love somebody with all your heart

and later have it all fall apart

to learn the feelings aren't the same

I was just a pawn in his game

he led me on to make me believe

that he was mine and would never leave

even now long after he has been gone

he still tries to lead me on

my heart never knew such pain

my days never saw so much rain

years of living with a love that will never be returned

I guess for me it will just be a lesson learned

but since my heart has grown so cold

I may never love as I grow old

love unreturned always last the longest

love is not for the weak just the strongest

how I feel or what he has done he doesn't know

but someday he will reap what he sows

© Reannon Smith,
Dedicated to Seven DFFD

My reason

When I feel I can't face another day,

nothing seems to go my way

when I have those days of doubt

my kids remind me what life's about

they are the reason I breath and smile through the pain

they are my sunshine when all there is, is rain

they are my heartbeat and I'm the only parent they got

my children are the light that gets me through when I

feel I can not

Nature

Colorfully changing

seasons rearranging

mysteriously displaying

We salute you

Today is the day of remembrance to honor all that you do

you sacrifice your life for millions you never knew

even though a day is not nearly enough for what you put on the line

but we honor the great and our freedom is what you define

only you know the true battle it takes to make this the land of the free

and the visions of tragedy left scarred that you had to see

it takes strength and bravery to leave this country and fight as long as

you soldiers do

and I thank God everyday for the freedom you've given me, I'm honored

and I proudly salute you

for those who fought so we may be free

Welcome to Wonderland

Welcome to Wonderland, a place you have never seen

it's not a dream or reality we are somewhere in between

it's a place of so much wonder you must go explore

things I am sure you've only dreamed about before

things might look crazy, or slightly off, but I guarantee

that you will enjoy everything you see

so enjoy a cup of tea, try on a hat or two

as Wonderland welcomes you

Unbreakable

I am very optimistic

refuse to be another statistic

no matter how bad things are

they could be worse by far

I'm not in the hospital or in jail

I wake up every morning quite well

I have two wonderful blessings that keep my spirits high

so life can throw many reasons at me but they won't make me cry

© Reannon Smith, 16 days ago

untitled

I always knew you & I were never meant to be

and I am glad you found someone who makes you happy

it's still a little bittersweet to see you with someone steady

I just thought you would never be ready

my life won't be the same without you

but this is what I need to do

let you go like I tried so many times before

when I know I could find so much more

© Reannon Smith,
Dedicated to Seven DFFD

Time is delicate

Time is delicate, it goes by so fast

cherish every moment as if it were the last

time doesn't stand still

so make of it what you will

once it's gone you can't flip it over and start again like an hourglass

so don't let special memories come and pass

time is delicate and it will never slow down

so enjoy the time while you're still around

© Reannon Smith, 9 days ago

Just like daddy

When I grow up I am going to be just like my dad and hunt for deer

and have a farm where I will have my own herd of steer

wait until i get home and show daddy the buck I got today

pretty soon I will get a real one I'm getting bigger every day

I want to make my daddy proud and give him my buck

I think it will bring him good luck

I want to be just like my daddy and go hunting every day

and I know I will be good at it because he taught me his way

Undo it

Years ago I dreamt of my wedding day,

but that is far from my mind today

getting married someday was always my plan

but now my love has grown cold towards any man

I didn't see it coming how was I to know

that i would have feelings for him that would grow

I wasn't ready to fall it all happened so fast

I gave him my all and we didn't last

he strung me along for 5 long years

and many months of wasteful tears

the damage he done he put me through it

I was better before him I wish I could undo it

© *Reannon Smith,*

Dedicated to Seven DFFD

Serenity

The top of a mountain breathing in the fresh air

a beautiful serenity like this is very rare

green covered mountains, and water as far as the eye can see

sound of the waterfall and the cool breeze makes you feel free

the sepia colored water peach blueish sky

it's the perfect natural high

it's the closest to heaven, you will ever be

this is the perfect place for complete serenity

© Reannon Smith, 4 days ago

picture prompt

I wonder

When I am alone with my thoughts I think of you

I think of us and wonder if you want the same thing to

I'm not getting younger and time is a valuable thing

but I want more from you than just a fling

In the same way, love has been unkind to me

in ways of unfaithfulness and dishonesty

You and I are no strangers, I can be comfortable around you

but sometimes I wonder if you only knew?

© Reannon Smith,

Dedicated to Seven DFFD

I melt

Star struck people have nothing on you

their panics are mild compared to what I do

there is no doubt when you are around or I hear your name

the feelings, emotions, that overwhelm are all the same

I am at a loss for words I can't move but want to run and hide

I lose my breath like dropping from the top of a roller coaster ride

I lose all sense of reality,

and to tell you honestly

I don't know how you make me do the things that I do

but I melt at anything that has to do with you.

© Reannon Smith

Dedicated to Seven DFFD

Bad Girls

Cowboys around here aren't the only ones who carry a gun

I maybe a cowgirl who doesn't work in a brothel nor am I an

outlaw on the run

Law is always hard to come by in this side of town

it is where most outlaws hang around

I have had a few run-ins where I had to pull my six shooter from my

side

I am not the damsel in distress when something goes down I run and

hide

Some folks call me a bad girl because I carry a gun

but that won't stop me my job around here ain't done

Yeah I sit at the bar and have a shot of whiskey or two

that's what most cow folks 'round here do

I ride in the night on my horse named Midnight

I help make sure folks around here act right

© Reannon Smith, 2 days ago

prompt wild wild west

Do I wanna know

My words that maybe only you can understand

is this feeling flowing together I need to know firsthand

nights are made for drinking and words are expressed more freely

I'm always at the edge I just want kiss you really

you are a drug I can't live without and I'm on my knees always crawling

back to you

so I really got to know if it is just me or are you feeling the same way to

hate to see you go but love seeing you walk away

all reality I am begging you to stay

© R.Smith, Dedicated to Seven DFFD

96 words Arctic Monkeys- do i wanna know

F5

The blue skies turn dark gray

a storm is heading your way

winds start picking up speed, then the alarm sound

the power goes out, it's time to take shelter underground

I began only being 250 feet wide

but as I get bigger there's nowhere to hide

at my biggest I am now 3 miles wide

making destruction to all that I collide

foundations can't stop me

I swallow them so easily

a dark funnel spinning carrying vehicles buildings and more

I won't leave much behind that's for sure

winds at 300 mph they call me an F5

when I pass through I don't leave much alive

© *Reannon Smith, June 19th, 2015*

How could you

Once I fell there was no going back

now I'm hurting but I see what you lack

if I only knew before I fell

I wouldn't be sad as hell

you knew you had no intentions to catch me

why would you let it continue to be

for you to be hated, I could never do

all I can say is how could you.

Dedicated to Seven DFFD

"I don't hate you, I never could, I hate how you made me fall for you, when you knew

you had no intentions of catching me." --Rashida Rowe

It's still hard

I remember that look in your eyes when you glanced over at me

asking for forgiveness because you found love, that's easy to see

I know she must mean a lot your actions say it all

I barely get a reply back every time I call

I know you weren't the one I would spend the rest of my life

but every time I see you it just cuts me like a knife

I can't seem to shake you or get you off my mind

I have tried so hard, but it is you I always find

I will never be over it the scars will always show

and it hurts more than you will ever know

© *Reannon Smith, June 24th, 2015*

Dedicated to Seven DFFD

Her soul mate

The man that she will always love

an angel who resides above

he visits her in her dreams every night

on the hills with colors so bright

but that's only when

she's sees him again

Love picture prompt

35 words

Changing times

Back in the olden days

people were set in their ways

everything a meaning and only one

now society is coming undone

adding words that were never before

changing meanings and what for

forgetting what our ancestors fought and died for

and now they want to remove the confederate flag and more

if they are going to go this far why not just rewrite history as well

it is not hard to see this country has all gone to hell

we as americans have to stand up for what's right

do as our forefathers go to war and fight

they fought so we may live in the land of the free

blood was shed for our future they didn't give up so easily

we should not them them change what its originally known for

it was never a racial thing it was fought for during the war

that flag is a reminder of what was won in a war

lets do whats right this should not be ignored

Tainted

I never thought that I would be alone

without love doing everything on my own

Love has always gone wrong for me

now it's tainted and I don't care to be

it hurts to see couples everywhere

deep down I still really care

right now my two kids are my life

I don't have time to be somebody's wife

but someday they to will move on

then all that I love will forever be gone

Temptation (adult)

The flames of desire ignite

I want you now, all night

the passion we have together is so hot

resist you is what I can not

I would spend a lifetime in hell

because together we do it so well

come to me as I lay naked in bed

and let the fire of our passion spread

this is a temptation I can't resist and that is no lie

there is nothing hotter than the passion between you and I

picture prompt

I am my own worst enemy

I feel there is no cure

for all this hell I endure

I keep falling until I hit the ground

and when I look there is no one around

I only have myself to blame

for the things that I have became

until I can start seeing things clear

it is me who keeps putting me here

the only one to blame is me and me alone

I am only weeping what I have sown

the only time I can see things clearer

is when I look at myself in the mirror

this healing process is very slow

and these demons don't want to let go

in the end with all that I have to gain

a reminder of the scars will always remain

© Reannon Smith, June 26th, 2015

Linkin Park, Crawling song prompt

Learning about love

With time the pain of heartbreak eases

love can sometimes be our worst diseases

when things seem to always go wrong

and it feels that you and love don't get along

take the time to focus on you

really start thinking things through

look in the mirror, do you like what you see?

to find love, we must love ourselves completely

happiness starts with ourselves, from within

that is when a life of love will truly begin

the patterns of loss and heartbreak will cease

and you will find a love that gives you great peace

Love for life prompt.. the brighter side

All American Dog

when I was growing up we had a red nose pit

they are my favorite breed I will have to admit

too many times you are accused of being the vicious breed

but they don't realize it's the owners that plant that see

(chorus)

Pitbulls you are labeled as ferocious and mean

with your lock jaws tearing people to smithereens

it's not your fault because that's the way you were taught

are you a bad breed? no i think not

you do what you are suppose to, to protect your yard

you must have scared somebody catching them off guard

Pitbulls are the all American dog they show a lot of affection

but you get put down if you give your owner some protection

(chorus)

Pitbulls you are labeled as ferocious and mean

with your lock jaws tearing people to smithereens

it's not your fault because that's the way you were taught

are you a bad breed? no i think not

picture prompt write a song for a red nose pit

Death do us part

Love can be cruel and love can be kind

But this is the love he left behind

A couple that displayed the real meaning of love every day

Until a tragedy hit home taking him away

But they have a love that is so strong and pure

That not even death can keep him away from her

picture prompt 57 words

Night sky colored

July 4th we celebrate our country's birthday

and we celebrate in a mesmerizing way

with colors and loud bangs we light up the night sky

like a rocket taking off they shoot way up high

they dissipate like a falling star

they can been seen about anywhere you are

they burst into many colors and different shapes to

they sparkle like eyes that are colored blue

the grand finale makes the night sky seem like its day

and then a roar like a lion from the crowd cheering hooray

I think it's time to say goodbye

I think it's time we said goodbye

I don't think you have to ask why

the honeymoon is over and I guess so are we

telling you this is really hard for me

I thought you were the one but it seems you've drifted apart

sometimes I think you don't care when it's breaking my heart

all we do is argue and fight

we never lay with each other at night

you always called me by a pet name

but lately things aren't the same

I am sorry it has to end this way

but our relationship has seen better days

I think it's time we said goodbye

so we can still part with ours heads held high

© Reannon S. July 17th 2015

You're the few and far between

I can't say I was at first a fan

because I was in love with that man

I know I will never have what you two have together

we never had never will, no matter what come hither

when I first got your text I thought all your words were deceiving

when it comes to girls and ex's, something good is hard believing

but I see you are true to your word and who you are

and that is a rare quality for any girl by far

it is good to know that there really are honest girls like you

who aren't about drama and do what they say they are going to do

you have my utmost respect and I don't say that to anyone

then again I never met somebody who would do what you've done

I hope the best for the both of you

and things work out if you want it to

either way I wish you the best and I'm glad to say that I know you

because you are a person that has a quality that is only in so few

© Reannon S. July 17th 2015

To my left

I sit here in a cluttered small room

to my left I see in full fake bloom

colors that stand out of purple and white

held up by a pole underneath the light

with a fake stem and leaves of the perfect green

two dozen fake roses in this grungy scene

in this cornered off room in the garage where I sit

to my left are these fake roses in this scene they do not fit

© Reannon S. July 31st 2015 prompt look to your left

Love and love no more

You know that feeling that love brings

the warm butterflies in your stomach kinda thing

that kool-aid grin when you think of that one

a feeling so strong it can't be undone

what happens when one does not feel that way

keeps you around while they go out and play

the truth becomes nothing but lie after lie

and all their deceit will make you cry

© Reannon S. August 1st 2015

Actions say it all

You say I'm the only one and that you love me

I hear your words but it's far from what I see

when we first started you couldn't look away

now it's hard to keep you around to stay

you say I'm being foolish, you aren't going anywhere

words are easy to say when you don't really care

I physically show you that I care about you

but you pay no attention and have no clue

I caress your body every night

with a soft touch that's feathery light

but you keep your back towards me

and I'm not blind I can see

I know why you never answer when I call

talk is cheap and your actions say it all

© *Reannon S. August 3rd 2015*
Dedicated to Seven DFFD

Nobody's perfect

Love takes patience and an open mind

if you're looking for perfection it's not what you'll find tears of sadness may fall

but he didn't mean it at all

the mouth is quicker than the mind

and everyone has said something very unkind

he knows your pain and he'll be back to wipe your tears

just as he was by your side helping you face your fears

you know his gentleness in his hand

he is not like any other man

he's not going to leave you broken to pick up what's shattered

because to him you are all that really matters

nothing but god is perfect, there will be a time when everyone will hurt you

but you just have to feel who is it worth suffering through

© Reannon S. August 3rd 2015
The truth is everyone is going to hurt you. You just gotta find the ones worth
suffering for. -Bob Marley

What if? I would

I pondered the question very deep in thought
thinking long and hard I decided that I would not

nothing in the world can change the person I've come to be
I have to children and without them my life would be empty

my life hasn't been a breeze, I've hit rock bottom lost it all
I struggled with addiction and made it back over the wall

I would change bad decisions I had made in the past
I would cherish the moments that went by too fast

I wish these last five years were just a joke

because I haven't made past all the smoke

but to be given a chance to leave it behind and start over new

well for me that's impossible because it's something I'd never do

What if...you woke up today with nothing but a backpack, a plane ticket and a note??

Here's the note:

"You have been given the opportunity to do whatever you want to be doing in this moment with yourself, your life, and your dreams. You have NO restrictions, NO obligations, NOTHING in your way. No job, no kids, no school, no spouse, no daily responsibilities holding you back!!

So, this is your new life. Now, what the hell are you going to do with it??

You have yourself, your life, and your dreams. No past, no future, no worries, no regrets!! Only NOW!! Now it's time for YOU to live out your forgotten dreams or create new ones!!

Rewind

Both of my kids just had their birthday

eleven and twelve they are now

so grown up I just pray

I could rewind time somehow

it doesn't seem so very long ago

that they were only three and four

I can't believe how fast they grow

and every second I love them more

I'm sad because they aren't babies anymore

time flies and it doesn't stop or slow down

they are my world that's for sure

but right now i wear a frown

© Reannon S. August 13th 2015

I'm asking

Would you go with me

if I couldn't see

through the flames and the smoke

ao I know this is real and no joke

would you hold on to me so tight

so I would know that this was right

if I told you that I would die

if you weren't by my side

if I let you go

would you let me know

that you'd still go with me

and tie up the end of this dream

would you take my hand and forever be in my life

and make me happy by becoming my wife

do me a favor please

and go with me

© Reannon S. August 16th 2015
prompt #4 Would you go with me ~ Josh Turner

What hurts the most

I never intended on falling for you

I didn't think my heart would allow me to

if I would have known that we could never be

but now it's too late for my heart to see

you grew on me and before I knew

my heart was falling for you

this love is nothing time can heal

and even knowing you will never feel

the same for me or the pain I endure

a love I can't have, there is no cure

no matter what I do or what I try

I still want you no other guy

if you only knew this kind of pain

loving what you can't have drives a person insane

© *Reannon S. August 16th 2015*
"The greatest pain that comes from love is loving someone You can never have."

Life

Sometimes my emotions are more than I can take

I can't verbally express myself and I'm ready to break

the pen helps release all that I can't say

it tells the story about my day

if I'm happy, hurt, loved, or sad

I put it all on the pad

my poetry is basically my biography, the story of me

it is my raw emotion and it's not always something happy

I have had many struggles and doubts

and being lonely always left out

so I always turn to the paper and pen

poetry helps me so I don't keep it bottled in

It's Over

It's over, he broke up with her tonight
so she hides behind a tree on this rainy night

tears falling like the rain from the sky
feeling sick wondering why

where did it all go wrong
feeling like she don't belong

it's over and she is feeling the pain
alone at night, she hides in the rain

In the night

Even though he's gone, he comforts me at night

when I lay down to go to sleep and turn off the light

he whispers in my ear to give me peace of mind

everything's ok I shouldn't be so confined

even though I can't see him, his words are very clear

and it makes me ok even though he is not here

I still feel the hurt of losing him during the daylight

that's because he only whispers to me in the night

Evening sky

Any month of summer, you can look at the evening sky

the colors are majestic, like fireworks on fourth of July

I'm in California and it's so beautiful to see

somewhere overlooking the town is the best place to be

unless you live by the ocean then nothing's more

perfect than sitting on the beach

watching the sunset the sky turns violet purple, orange

then orange fades into peach

just the pastel colors in the evening sky is such a wonderful sight

listening to the rhythm of the waves makes for a perfect night

---

we don't have a harvest moon, cornfields or fireflies

but if you could see the beauty of the evening skies

Lying eyes

Back in the beginning things were so good

if I could only turn back time I would

but not to be the way we use to be

because it wasn't too long before you stopped loving me

now you say it with desperation in your eyes

knowing that what you said was nothing but lies

I know I'm not the only one

and I'm not going to come undone

is this the way you play your game

with no guilt and no shame

but you aren't the only one who has been telling a lie

and when it's over you won't see me cry

because I have been talking to your other friend

and soon your lies will all come to an end

© Reannon Smith, August 28th 2015

Bittersweet

It's hard to believe I will never hear the sound of your bike driving by

but why should I care ? all you ever did was make me cry

not with intentions or purposely but with your actions

because everything was always about your satisfaction

I had to be there while you were arm and arm with someone new

it was easy to see I never meant shit to you

so why do I wonder why do I still care

when it came to me, you were never there

I loved you so much and got strung along in return

but for you, my love still burns

Death becomes our youth

It more than one name, heroin, black, tar

it has become the biggest killer of youth by far

it's well known and very popular with the younger generation

and it's taking its toll of deaths in our nation

so many have no knowledge of this drug and rather look the other way

this epidemic is killing hundreds a day

we are losing so many at a young age because most have no clue about the sickness, craving, and pain that heroin can do

I, myself have known so many that died that could have been easily prevented,
but the knowledge known to people is usually misrepresented

it's devastating, and it's spreading like a wildfire it's time for people to get a
clue
because it might be too late if you think it can't happen to you

When it rains I see you

Lately when it rains I see you

and in my mind it's just us two

big shady trees and green grass in a park

walking side by side then the sky turns dark

as we look up the rain begins to come down

we know it's time to turn back around

before we can even get to take ten steps

it starts pouring and we're both soaking wet

as soon as I look at you and start to pick up the pace

you pull me toward you, your other hand on my face

like a scene from a movie we passionately kiss

things get hot and heavy and too good to resist

in the open but where no one else can see

your hands move and start to undress me

and right before we go down to our knees

I open my eyes and realize this is just my fantasy

Two paths

In life, there are two paths you can take

the decision is solely yours to make

the path to hell may seem like fun

do what you please, and answer to no one

you can fulfill every want and need

think wisely before you plant that seed

heaven promises to give you all your desires

without living in eternity in the pits of fire

believe in the good and live a prosperous life every day

in life there are two paths, you choose which way

© *Reannon Smith, September 19th 2015*

Losing it all

In the back of my mind, I'm still with you

but it's hard to pretend and I don't think I can continue

trying everything I could

hoping that you would

now everything's crashing down on me

and I don't think that I can break free

now I'm all alone, standing center stage

losing it all, but I can't turn the page

what it takes to be a man

It does not take much to be a real man
something boys will never understand

you don't have to be muscular or have
a lot of cash
at least be presentable don't come looking
like a piece of trash

be kind and admit your faults when you're wrong
a woman will be mad but not for very long

if you get a girl pregnant take your responsibility
and step up to the plate
promising you'll never leave and then bail will
get you a lot of hate

see what guys don't understand
simple things make a real man

© Reannon Smith, September 23rd, 2015

In the night

There is something that gets me curious

that the night can be so mysterious

how the moonlight can give a soft glow

or be modest and does not show

it gives off a glare of orange or grey

in the sky like a big ball clay

it can act as a spotlight

in the middle of the night

there is something calming about the night

and the way it is lit by the moonlight

© Reannon Smith, September 23rd, 2015

Solo

I guess he was not meant to be

at least he was not meant for me

I am no stranger to this road I walk alone

sadden by love, my heart is now of stone

I have been on this path so many times

and still I wonder but only sometimes

is there someone out there waiting for me

or is walking solo the way it will always be

Hello Autumn

Hello Autumn it's nice to have you here
soon the green leaves will disappear

changing colors to red, orange and brown
of leaves that will soon fall to the ground

bringing the smell of warm pumpkin pie
and more of the stars and nighttime sky

cooling down the heat from the summer sun
as children get excited, for Halloween fun

families start planning for the thanksgiving meal
autumn always bring a warm and cozy feel

like the soft whistling wind in the night
the orange harvest moon with a soft light

the taste of turkey dinners and Halloween sweets

autumn brings out the best of good eats

hello autumn it's nice to have you here

soon the summer heat will disappear

Moments

You never know if the people that you meet

live in a house, apartment or on the street

yet most are quick to judge, labeling them a bum

thinking that they are lazy or plain dumb

nobody chooses this lifestyle or are they born this way

they once lived like most everyone else until it was taken away

they've had their moments with a home and a family

moments that were suddenly taken by a tragedy

don't be quick to judge they haven't always been this way

they once had their moments when they worked every day

so never make judgement it's not your call

because you don't know how they lost it all

One on One

People today talk a lot of shit

when confronted, can't back it

there was such a time ago

when people went toe to toe

outside, one on one

now those days are done

now it's all talk, run and hide

or have a group at your side

so tell me sup

it's time to man up,

let's go head to head

for the shit you said

outside one on one

non-stop until we're done

music prompt song is Take it outside by Brantley Gilbert

No regrets

If your heart seeks it, you should try

we never know when it's our time to die

seek out what makes you a free soul

it's never too late to reach your goal

do what you've always wanted to do

never let anything ever stop you

dance in the rain let your heart sing

let your free spirit do anything

love like that's all you know

never let a chance go

always be quick to forgive and forget

never live with any regret

if it's in your soul then it's meant to do

never die with music still inside you

© *Reannon Smith, October 1st, 2015*

Deceived

I thought that he loved me, but I was deceived

anything and everything he said to me I believed

he said he loved me, but I know now he lied

his fork in tongue, he lured me to the dark side

and in a moment he turned my life upside down

and made sure I had nobody that would be around

he made sure I dug a hole too deep to get out alone

and just like that he was gone, a heart of stone

I lost everything I worked so hard to get,

but this is something I will never forget

my kids my family I was on my own

struggling to get out all alone

it has been 5 years since that fateful day

and I am never going to love a man in any way

he broke me I have lost my trust he took all I have achieved

because I loved someone, but I was only being deceived

© Reannon Smith, October 2nd, 2015

Born Again

I was sitting here the other

day and I saw a light

so I opened my heart

and I got right

a voice told me, worry no

more I know the way

I know I found

GOD that day

ever since then I feel

a weight has been lifted

I have a sense of freedom

like my life's been shifted

but I still pray to have

my kids back again

he said, child just

confess all of your sins

since you finally found

the path of the right

you know I am the way

and I am the light

and as I hear myself

confess all my sins

a tear falls from my face and

I know I'll have my kids back again

and I thank all my family for all

their prayers for me at night

and the patience of GOD

waiting on me to see the light

© Reannon Smith October 2nd 2015

This too shall pass

In our darkest moments

and biggest storms,

out of nowhere a bright

light will suddenly form

keep faith and he will always

keep light from the candle

for the Lord will never put

you through what you can't handle

he is our light and the way

he's what the world needs today

so when you feel all is lost and

you can't take anymore,

call upon him, just bow your

head as your knees hit the floor

© Reannon Smith, October 6th 2015

A United Community

In a small community,

in the midst of a tragedy

without blame, instead whether

united they came together

still strong in their beliefs

even during this time of grief

a town full of heart for all who reside

united compassion and pride

they show the true beauty of a community

that have a bond as strong as family

Roseburg, Oregon is a place of love

and with this, they will still rise above

Just one wish

One thing I wish for
is to be scared no more

even though I know things
won't go my way
just to have the courage to
look at you and say

before we broke up I
never knew
and still to this day
"I love you"

© Reannon Smith, October 11th, 2015

Sinner's salvation

Some of us may veer down the wrong path

and it's not long before you feel the wrath

miracles happen, second chances are given
and only by God you are still living

he knows your heart and what you will do
a chance to become the better you

give life, teach and follow his word
there is no voice that isn't unheard

the only one that didn't die that day
a sinner's salvation one might say

if you go to the church the story will be told
of the 3 wooden crosses on the side of the road

© Reannon Smith, October 13th, 2015

Different approach

I pour my heart out for you

and what good does that do

maybe I have been going

about it the wrong way,

let's talk about why you

had to go astray!

I've heard all your lies

and they're getting old

it's time for the truth

to be told

you broke my heart and

you made me cry

so now is the time to explain

to me why?

was I a challenge in the

game you play

that's why it was so

easy to walk away

tell me, did I rise to the challenge

and give you a good game

or in the end are we all

just the same

do you care about anyone

else besides you?

I guess that's why you can

do the things you do

I still love you, I just stay

blind to what is real

but i can't keep my eyes closed

forever, it's time for me to heal

it's time I face the truth and

look you in the eye's

and stop hanging on to all

of your lies

but I will always love you and

be your friend til the end of time

it just wasn't meant for us to be

life long partners in crime

© Reannon Smith October 15th 2015

there comes a time when you have to believe what you already know and

take that step and let go. healing is the process of feeling

Unknown

Unknowing time of death

never taking that chance

keep living with regrets

not knowing what could have been

or what should have been

wondering if it could have been you

not knowing the unexpected but its life

© Reannon Smith October 21st 2015

Prayers from Heaven

There wasn't any sign that he was going to go

but he's praying in heaven and wants you to know

right now it is hard to understand

the reason for God's greater plan

and even though we may never know

why someone has to suddenly go

it is by God and the power of prayer

to find peace when he's not there

even though our loved ones had died

they are always there silently by our side

every day the sun will shine, but the pain is still new

I pray you find peace and know he is still with you

Broken Angel

no more waiting,

the light burned out

and so did my heart

It's over

I sit here in the misty dusk at the end of the pier

the endless view of the blue lake is the crystal clear

I hear the crashing waves coming up on the shore,

but there is a sense of silence that's hard to ignore.

somethings are hard to swallow, as a tear rolls down my face

a chill runs down my body I'm reminded of your embrace

and tonight on this pier I sit here alone

I still smell the fragrance of your cologne

but all my love for you just wasn't enough

because you walked out when things got rough

I guess it's safe to say, you didn't feel the same way

from dusk til dawn I'll be sitting alone on this pier

it's chilly and foggy, but it helps me think clear

I thought we'd be forever you were the perfect guy,

but it's over and I'm trying to understand why

© Reannon Smith November 4th 2015

Free

today she let it all go

she's happy and free

today she let it all go

and amazing is she

wearing colors so bold and bright

no longer wearing colors of the night

she let it all go and danced in the rain

complete happiness is what she gained

© Reannon Smith November 6th 2015

Born Again

I was sitting here the other

day and I saw a light

so I opened my heart

and I got right

a voice told me, worry no

more I know the way

I know I found

GOD that day

ever since then I feel

a weight has been lifted

I have a sense of freedom

like my life's been shifted

but I still pray to have

my kids back again

he said, child just

confess all of your sins

since you finally found

the path of the right

you know I am the way

and I am the light

and as I hear myself

confess all my sins

a tear falls from my face and

I know I'll have my kids back again

and I thank all my family for all

their prayers for me at night

and the patience of GOD

waiting on me to see the light

© *Reannon Smith October 2nd 2015*

artist at his best

an illusion is at the eye of the beholder

you think you could reach out and hold her?

he brought to life a picture he painted on a wall

and if anything is real you couldn't tell at all

39 words

Senseless

Today in my home town families were destroyed for good

By people with no conscious because they thought they could

The devil is on the loose and destroying as much as he can

California is one nation UNDER GOD and United we will stand

today's shooting in San Bernardino, CA happened about 10 min from where I live and

the shoot out with these terrorists happened a block from my work

Stranded

it's dark, the moon is full, leaning against the post

dark angel to him you are nothing but a ghost

CPSIA information can be obtained
at www.ICGtesting.com
Printed in the USA
BVHW080802261221
624839BV00018B/602